COOKABILITY

with Keith Kenny

AMAZING RECIPES

that have been adapted for

GLUTEN AND DAIRY FREE COOKING

Photography by Jocasta Clarke

BLACKWATER PRESS

CONTENTS

Acknowledgements

I would like to thank Melanie D'Arcy-Kenny for sharing life with me and supporting all my endeavours, both good and bad.

Special thanks to Jocasta Clarke for being the best food photographer bar none and putting in so much time, and to Sean Maguire for the additional help. Also to Feargal Duffy for acting as any good wingman should, telling me when I was wrong and not praising me too much when I was right!

To my staff, Danny, Brian, Julie, Marcel and Milly whose help in preparing the dishes was invaluable.

To Erika Doolan who knows more about food than anybody else and provided her valuable expertise at such short notice on Nutritional Information.

To John O'Connor who, after a chance meeting and a brief conversation, gave me the opportunity to publish this book and to Paula Byrne for being the guiding hand in designing it.

My suppliers Alan Hegarty and Niall Collins and to everybody else who helped me get this book over the line.

Food Philosophy

Fresh, fresh, fresh, buy local and don't be afraid to experiment.

I'd particularly like to thank you for buying this book as you are helping others. All my royalties from this book are being donated to the Irish Cancer Society and the fantastic work they do in Ireland.

The Irish Cancer Society is Ireland's national cancer charity. The Society provides information, support and care to those with, and affected by, cancer all over Ireland. Its services are professional, confidential and free of charge. The Society is almost entirely funded through the generosity of the public and receives less than five per cent government funding.

Visit www.cancer.ie for more information.

Dedication

This book is dedicated to Mary Lawlor, Breda Kenny
and Jack & Betty D'Arcy and to all families
who have been touched by cancer.

Introduction

Why did I write a gluten-free, dairy-free and coeliac-friendly cookbook I hear you ask?

OK, you didn't ask, but as you're reading this I'm going to tell you anyway!

As a chef and restaurateur, I am well aware of the difficulties that can be faced when going out for a meal with friends or family. If you are the only one on a special diet and mention any of the above dietary requirements, you are frequently met with a raised eyebrow from the waiter and then get a hastily arranged bland salad thrust under your nose. Unfortunately, I have had personal experience of such dining disasters as my wife, Melanie, is dairy and gluten intolerant and is usually limited to completely bland unimaginative meals.

When I first opened my own restaurant, La Banca in Lucan, County Dublin, I made it my goal to create a menu that anyone would be able to enjoy. All of the dishes are frequently adapted to suit gluten-free, dairy-free or coeliac-friendly diets. I invite our customers to share with us their particular needs so that every freshly prepared dish can be created to suit every dietary requirement.

For someone who has spent his entire life in a kitchen, this has proven to be one of the most exciting and professionally demanding things I have ever done as I change the specials on a daily basis and rewrite the entire menu on a monthly basis.

Good chefs like to be challenged, but the best chefs are those who accept the challenges. So the next time you are out for a meal, tell them what **you** would like to eat and if they have an ounce of passion or imagination about food, they will be only too delighted to oblige and do something different.

This book is not just by a chef but by someone who understands the restrictions and difficulties faced on a daily basis by those with dietary restrictions. My culinary imagination was opened to a whole new way of cooking and array of ingredients that I never used in a domestic or commercial kitchen. So thanks again Melanie!

Hence, the name of my book is *Cookability*. I have created down to earth easy-to-follow recipes as I want to give you the ability and confidence to cook these delicious dishes without being restricted.

Thank you for buying my book and I really hope you will enjoy the recipes and please let me know how you get on.

All the Best,

Keith Kenny

About Food Intolerances — ERIKA DOOLAN

Gluten

Gluten is a protein that is found in wheat, spelt, kamut, barley, rye and sometimes oats (oats are more often contaminated with gluten). The immune system in people who are either coeliac positive or gluten sensitive perceives gluten as a foreign invader. This leads to an activation of the immune cells in the intestines when exposed to gluten. These immune cells release chemicals that can lead to the destruction of the surface, or villi, of the intestines. When the intestinal villi are damaged, there is an inability to absorb nutrients from food. This often leads to malnutrition conditions that can be triggered by pregnancy, childbirth, viral infections, severe emotional stress or even after routine surgery.

Coeliac disease is a growing problem in Ireland affecting more than 1 in 100 people. For more information on gluten-free food and lifestyle and financial support in Ireland check out www.coeliac.ie

There are lots of gluten-free foods on shop shelves that contain a lot of junk and are high in sugar. Instead of buying these, I recommend you stick with wholesome foods that are naturally gluten-free like fresh fruits and vegetables, fish, chicken, lean meat, beans, lentils, brown or wild rice, low-fat dairy, nuts, seeds, olive oil and gluten-free flours. There are so many things that are naturally gluten-free.

I have seen that most cases of chronic diarrhoea, arthritis, chronic fatigue and irritable bowel disease are associated with gluten sensitivity. When my clients transition to eating foods free of gluten, most of these conditions either disappear entirely or improve considerably. Coeliacs are always low in iron and can be very sick, in pain, swollen stomach and lose weight.

Coeliac disease and gluten sensitivity symptoms:

- Gas
- Recurring abdominal bloating and pain
- Chronic diarrhoea
- Nausea with or without vomiting
- Acid reflux
- Weight loss / weight gain
- Fatigue
- Unexplained anaemia
- Bone or joint pain
- Osteoporosis
- Behavioural changes
- Tingling numbness in the legs from nerve damage
- Muscle cramps
- Seizures
- Missed menstrual periods
- Infertility / reoccurring miscarriages
- Delayed growth
- Failure to thrive in infants
- Pale sores inside mouth
- Tooth discolouration or loss of enamel
- Dermatitis

Gluten is found everywhere in our food supply. Baking powder can contain gluten. So can pasta, cottage cheese, soy sauce, beer and marshmallows. In addition, non-food sources of gluten include the adhesives on stamps and envelopes. Adhering to a gluten-free diet can be challenging. Over 90% of my clients who consume a gluten-free diet still consume a small source of gluten without ever knowing it. It often requires a thorough diet diary evaluation to find all the potential pitfall foods. Once these foods are replaced in a gluten sensitive person, changes in health are often seen immediately.

Hidden Food Sources:

- Baking powder
- Beer
- Bread
- Brown rice syrup
- Sweets
- Caramel colour
- Cereal
- Citric Acid
- Coffee (flavoured)
- Dairy products: modified starch in yoghurts, cottage cheese, chocolate
- Dextrin: can be made from wheat
- Flavourings: meat flavourings may contain wheat
- Flour
- Grains
- Malt: if made from barley
- Maltodextrin
- Meat: Fillers in processed meats
- Miso: barley
- Modified Food Starch
- Non-dairy milk
- Oatmeal
- Packaged dessert mixes
- Pastas
- Seasoning
- Soups
- Soy sauce
- Vegetable starch
- Vinegar: except wine vinegars, brown rice vinegars and apple cider vinegar
- Yeast

Go through your cupboard and discard any old whole grain flours as they can spoil easily. The oils found in the germ and bran of wholegrains can go rancid quite easily when ground into flours. Store your wholegrain flours in the refrigerator or freezer if you will not be using them right away. Brown rice flour, buckwheat flour, teff flour, millet flour, quinoa flour, amaranth flour, sorghum flour and tapioca flour are naturally gluten-free. Be sure to look for a gluten-free symbol on the label as some flours may be processed in the same facility as gluten containing flours and therefore be cross-contaminated.

Buckwheat Flour

The packaged buckwheat flour you buy in the store is ground from roasted buckwheat groats, so it has a very strong robust flavour. You may also grind your own from raw buckwheat groats. They grind up very quickly to a fine powder in a coffee grinder, and even faster if you own a grain grinder. Buckwheat flour makes a delicious pancake and can also be used to make muffins, quick breads and some desserts.

Teff Flour

Teff is so tiny that the entire grain is milled leaving all the nutrients intact. Teff flour is highly nutritious, being particularly high in iron, protein, fibre and complex carbohydrates. The rich buttery flavour of teff flour makes an ideal addition to most baked goods. Use it to make pancakes, brownies, biscuits, yeast breads, quick breads and more. You can mix half of the brown rice flour with teff flour for ultimate results.

Brown Rice Flour

Brown rice flour is a staple gluten-free baking flour in my house. Its subtle flavour makes an ideal base for cakes, breads, muffins and desserts. For more nutrient-dense baked goods, substitute half or more of the brown rice flour with teff, sorghum, buckwheat, quinoa or amaranth flour.

Millet Flour

Millet flour's light yellow colour and sweet flavour work well in cakes, quick breads and muffins. Millet is a versatile grain, mildly sweet and nutty and it can be used in everything. It continues to be a staple for a third of the world's population. A huge interest in the grain has been growing, especially in gluten-free diets. Millet is nutritious, providing fibre, iron, B vitamins, manganese, phosphorus and magnesium, and it is extremely alkaline, making it easily digestible and soothing to the stomach.

Quinoa Flour

Quinoa flour has a strong flavour and should be used in combination with other mild flours such as brown rice flour. Quinoa flour is very high in protein making it a great addition to quick breads and muffins.

Amaranth Flour

Amaranth flour has a distinct, sweet, nutty flavour, though it can sometimes leave a bitter aftertaste. It is high in protein and iron and can be used in combination with other flours in baking. Excellent for waffles, pancakes, quick breads, biscuits and muffins.

Sorghum Flour

Sorghum flour adds delicious flavour and texture to gluten-free baked goods. It is a good substitute for whole wheat flour, as it has a familiar taste and texture.

Tapioca Flour

Tapioca flour comes from the ground starch of the cassava root. A small part of tapioca flour is used in combination with other gluten-free flours in baked goods to help them stick together. Gluten and egg-free baked goods made without tapioca flour may crumble and fall apart once baked.

Not all wheat is bad for us . . . for example, spelt and kamut have a much lower gluten content, and now we can buy them in health food shops as flour, bread and pasta. Research proves that a large percentage of dietary starch, such as wheat, escapes absorption in the small intestines. This wheat is then completely digested by bacteria living in your intestines! This actually produces the various gases, causing bloating and flatulence. If you suffer from any of these symptoms why not try cutting wheat out of your diet completely for approximately two weeks? See what happens . . . you can continue eating grains like spelt, millet, kamut and quinoa. After two weeks reintroduce the wheat back into your diet . . . eat lots of it and see what happens. If this shows you that wheat is causing bloating and flatulence for you, reduce it as much as possible and in time if you will be able to have it occasionally without causing any problems.

The nutritional benefits of wholegrains are huge. Even small amounts per day can help reduce your risk of some of the biggest health epidemics such as heart disease, diabetes, stroke, a wide range of cancers, osteoporosis, hypertension and obesity. It is generally accepted the more wholegrains you eat, the more protected you are. It takes time to learn how to cook wholegrains so don't make the transition overnight. Change your habits over time and introduce these new wholesome flours gradually. In time, you can increasingly substitute whole grains such as amaranth, for the refined grains you are currently eating, such as white rice and pastas made from refined flours. Take action now and be mindful of what you and your family are consuming.

Dairy

For many years, cow's milk has been advertised as being essential for healthy bones and we were told to drink up from a very young age and some of us from birth. Cow's milk is designed for an entirely different species of animal, and therefore it is no surprise that a proportion of the population have adverse reactions when consuming it. Beyond the majority of the world's population that are lactose (milk and sugar) intolerant, many people also have various reactions to the proteins in cow's milk. There are at least 30 antigenic primary proteins in milk. Casein is the most commonly used milk protein in the food industry: lactalbumin, lactoglobulin, bovine albumin and gamma globulin are other protein groups within milk. Milk proteins are listed on food labels with a variety of names such as milk solids, skim milk powder, casein, whey and albumin.

The potential side effects of cow's formula have been well documented and can contribute to cases of eczema, colic, diarrhoea, and sinus conditions in infants. When breastfeeding mothers consume dairy products, their exclusively breast–fed children may test positive to having a cow's milk protein immune reactions. Later in life, a cow's milk sensitivity can contribute to sinus conditions, asthma, eczema, headaches, arthritis, acid reflux, constipation and other bowel problems. This does not apply to everyone however, if your child is suffering with allergies or unexplained symptoms it would be wise to take your child off all dairy for a period. For example, for an infant you could take them off dairy products for a period of 10 weeks and gradually, monitor and record a reintroduction of dairy products to identify the exact intolerance and a GP or nutritionist can help with this.

Look out for the following symptoms of dairy intolerance:

- Gas
- Abdominal bloating and pain
- Diarrhoea
- Constipation
- Gastrointestinal bleeding
- Anaemia
- Nausea and vomiting
- Acid reflux
- Chronic headaches /migraines
- Joint pain / arthritis
- Rhinitis
- Ear infections
- Hay fever
- Asthma
- Eczema
- Depression and mood swings
- ADHD
- Bedwetting in children

In my practice, I have seen that eliminating or reducing dairy products for some of my clients, can help resolve health conditions without use of medications. To get a test to determine if you react to dairy or you are lactose intolerant, ask your general practitioner or nutritional therapist to guide you in the right direction.

Non-Dairy Milk

Non-dairy milks come in many flavours such as plain, vanilla, chocolate and carob and can be found in cartons on the shelf of your local health food store and now in many grocery stores. Keeping a few different types of non-dairy milk in your cupboard to substitute milk will be helpful in getting you started. If you are gluten sensitive then sure to purchase a gluten-free rice or soy milk. Some brands contain a very small percentage of barley, malt or wheat so check the label.

Rice Milk

Rice milk is made from brown rice, water, sea salt and usually a small amount of oil. It is a very light, sweet tasting beverage that can replace cow's milk in most recipes. It has a high glycaemic load meaning it will spike your insulin. Use in dairy-free recipes but avoid drinking too much of this regularly.

Almond Milk

Almond milk is made by blending together a mixture of almonds, water, sea salt and usually some type of sugar or sweetener. It works well as a substitute for cow's milk in mainly baked recipes. It's actually mostly water by weight which means one cup of almond milk only contains the equivalent of about 4-5 almonds. Look for unsweetened almond milk, this is *very healthy* and is a low calorie beverage. It contains approximately 40 calories per cup and it's a terrific non-dairy choice for people who are vegan, have dairy allergies or are just looking to change things in their cereal or coffee. Most almond milks are fortified with the same amount of calcium and vitamin D that you find in cow's milk, therefore you still get those bone-building nutrients in your milk beverage. Compared to other milks, almond milk is significantly lower in protein. There's only about 1 gram per cup compared to dairy milk which has 8 grams per cup and soy milk which delivers 6-7 grams of protein per cup. Be wary of the sweetened varieties as these can be more like a dessert than a milk beverage. A cup of sweetened vanilla has about four teaspoons of sugar. One cup contains five teaspoons of sugar. It is basically another rich hot cocoa without the whipped cream and of course all that extra sugar means extra calories.

Boost your immune system and make a delicious, warming drink on a winter's evening. Simmer with spices such as cinnamon, cloves and ginger.

Hemp Milk

Hemp milk is a thick, rich, non-dairy milk made from hemp seeds, water and brown rice syrup. For the ultimate flavour and nutrition, hemp milk is my favourite blend. It is rich in healthy omega 3 fatty acids, protein and essential vitamins and minerals. Because of its high nutrient content I recommend it almost exclusively where non-dairy milk is required.

Soy Milk

Soy milk is made by grinding soybeans, mixing with water and cooking. The liquid is then pressed from the solids and filtered. Soy milk can be found unsweetened, sweetened or in flavours like vanilla and chocolate.

Coconut Milk

Coconut milk is excellent for the immune system. Kara coconut milk is a delicious brand and can be used as a milk alternative in cereals and in hot beverages. Coconut milk is extraordinarily versatile and serves a variety of purposes in the kitchen. From breakfast to dinner, savoury to sweet, coconut milk has a place in your diet. It is packed with vitamins C, E, B1, B3, B5, and B6 as well as iron, selenium, sodium, calcium, magnesium and phosphorus. And its benefits don't end in the gut. When you buy coconut milk, don't get a reduced fat version as many of coconut's renowned health properties are found in the fat. Many people are afraid to eat good fats but we need good fats to burn fat! Always keep a few cans of coconut milk in your cupboard for making quick curries, soups, and even homemade ice pops.

Erika Doolan

Soups, Snacks
Salads and Sauces

Chicken Noodle Soup
(Serves Four to Six)

Ingredients:

1 skinless breast of chicken

1 carrot, diced

1 courgette, diced

4 chestnut mushrooms, cut into quarters

1 chilli, diced with seeds left in

1 red or green bell pepper, diced

2 cloves of garlic, diced

1 cube of fresh ginger, diced

Juice of ½ lime

1 tbsp. soy sauce

1 stick celery, diced

1 tsp. oyster sauce

2 sprigs of coriander, chopped

100g rice noodles

4 baby sweetcorn

2 litres of chicken stock (just add 2 chicken stock cubes to boiling water)

Spring onions

Salt and pepper

Method:

Cut chicken into same sized small pieces as the vegetables. Put 2 litres of chicken stock in a medium sized pot and add all the vegetables, chicken, lime juice, soy and oyster sauces, garlic and ginger. Bring to a simmer and leave for 15 mins before adding the rice noodles and cooking until soft, usually 4-5 mins.

To serve, put in a bowl with chopped coriander and finely sliced spring onions.

Butternut Squash and Coconut Soup
(Serves Five to Six)

Ingredients:

1 butternut squash

2 medium sized carrots

1 medium sized onion

Juice of ½ lime

1 chilli, diced leaving the seeds in

400ml coconut milk (full fat)

3 tbps. of olive oil

2 chicken or vegetable stock cubes

Salt and pepper

Method:

First prepare your squash by removing the top and bottom ends of the squash. Then cut the body from the neck of the squash and then cut the body in two. Scoop out the seeds with a spoon and rinse away any excess pulp and put seeds aside in a bowl for later.

Don't peel your squash. Chop your squash, onion and carrots into cubes of roughly the same size. Dice your chilli.

Preheat a large pot and add 3 tbsp. of olive oil on a high heat. Throw all the veg into the pot with a pinch of salt and pepper along with the lime juice. Crumble in two chicken stock cubes and sauté the flavours together for 3 to 4 mins.

Add 1½ litres of boiling water and leave to simmer for 15 minutes, or until all vegetables are soft. If the liquid is reduced, just add another ½ litre of boiling water. Add most of the coconut milk, saving a small drop for garnishing, stir and bring back to boil before removing from heat. Blitz soup with a hand blender or food processor until you achieve a smooth consistency. Season to taste and serve.

The garnish

Put a tsp. of olive oil into a frying pan and throw in the butternut seeds with a pinch of salt. Sauté on a high heat for 2 to 3 minutes until they turn golden brown and leave aside for a couple of minutes. Don't overheat the pan or they'll pop like popcorn.

Pour soup into a bowl and, with a small dessert spoon, just add a small drop of your coconut milk and dribble down the centre of the soup. Dry seeds off on kitchen paper before garnishing on the soup.

Rustic Minestrone Soup
(Serves Five to Six)

Ingredients:

1 large carrot

1 medium sized onion

1 courgette

1 green pepper

1 red pepper

4 sticks of celery

3 cloves of garlic

4 baby sweetcorn

8 sugar snaps/peas

4 medium sized chestnut mushrooms

1 small sweet potato

Bunch of fresh basil

Juice of 1 lemon

1 tbsp. honey or sugar

2 tins chopped tomatoes

150g of gluten-free penne pasta (pre-cooked)

1 chicken or vegetable stock cube

3 tbsp. of olive oil

Salt and peper

Method:

This is an ideal brunch soup with lots of flavour and is quite filling.

Roughly dice all the veg into 1 cm square pieces, apart from the mushrooms, sweetcorn and sugar snap peas.

Put a medium sized pot on high heat with 3 tbsp. of olive oil and throw in all chopped veg. Crumble a dried stock cube into the pot along with a pinch of salt and pepper. Reduce to a medium heat and sauté for 4-5 mins, stirring regularly.

Add the two tins of chopped tomatoes and 2 litres of boiling water. Add the juice of ½ lemon and a tbsp. of honey, leaving to simmer for 10 minutes. While simmering, tear some leaves from a bunch of fresh basil. Cut the mushrooms into quarters and throw into pot before simmering for another 10 mins. Slice the sweetcorn and sugarsnaps into 2 cm strips, add to pot and simmer for another 2 mins.

It is important not to overcook the vegetables so taste periodically to ensure they are still *al dente* and add extra seasoning if required.

Place two cooked tbsp. of the cold, cooked pasta into a bowl and spoon out the minestrone soup on top, garnishing with a spring of basil.

On a cold day you can also add 2-3 splashes of tabasco sauce for extra heat.

Mushroom Soup with Mushroom Duxelles
(Serves Four to Six)

Ingredients:

For the soup

800g of wide cap field mushrooms or button mushrooms, sliced

2 tbsp. of olive oil

1 medium onion, diced

1 clove of garlic, diced

Juice of 1 lemon

1 litre of chicken or vegetable stock

2 sprigs of fresh dill, chopped

Salt and pepper

Method:

Heat the olive oil in a pot and add the onion, garlic and mushrooms, leaving to sweat off for 4-5 mins. Add in the lemon juice and stock and boil for a further 4-5 mins.

Blend all in a food processor until smooth and, if the soup is too thick, just add some more stock.

Add fresh dill, salt and pepper to taste.

Ingredients:

For the Duxelles

8–10 wide cap field mushrooms or button mushroom (or Morels mushrooms are really good in this too)

2 tbsp. of olive oil

1 shallot or ½ a medium sized onion, finely chopped

Salt and pepper

1 sprig of fresh thyme leaves

Method:

Put a pan on to heat and add the olive oil. When hot, add the mushrooms, onions, thyme and season, frying for 2-3 mins. Then blend until smooth in a food processor and garnish the top of the soup with a tsp. of duxelles as it adds an extra mushroom kick.

Roasted Red Pepper and Tomato Soup
(Serves Four to Six)

Ingredients:

2 tins chopped tomatoes

1 tbsp. tomato purée

Bunch of fresh basil

2 cloves of garlic, roughly chopped

1 tsp. honey

2 sticks of celery, roughly chopped

1 onion, roughly chopped

2 red peppers

2 tbsp. rapeseed or vegetable oil

½ litre of vegetable or chicken stock

Salt and pepper

Method:

To roast the red peppers, rub them with vegetable oil and then place in a pan that's been preheated on a high heat. Place and cook all the way around until the pepper is completely black. You can also do this blackening under the grill or in the oven.

When black, place into a bowl and cover with clingfilm. When cooled, remove skin, deseed and roughly chop.

Put a pot on a medium to high heat before adding 1 tbsp. of oil, onion, celery, red pepper, garlic and cook for 3-4 mins, then add the chopped tomatoes and stock, leaving to simmer gently for 25-30 mins.

Stir occasionally and add water if necessary. Transfer to a food processor along with the tomato purée and honey and blend until smooth. Return the soup to the pot with 6-8 basil leaves and simmer for another 4-5 mins before seasoning with salt and pepper for taste and serve hot.

TOMATO PASTE: If you have left over tomato paste, put it onto tablespoons and freeze before transferring to a labelled freezer bag. Hey tomato pesto, ready to use measured quantities for future recipes!

ROASTED RED PEPPER AND TOMATO SOUP

Chilli Hummus

Ingredients:

2 tins of chick peas, strained

1 fresh chilli or birds eye chilli if you like a real kick, finely chopped

4 cloves of garlic, peeled and finely chopped

Juice of 1 lime

Juice of 1 lemon

2 tbsp. of roasted sesame seeds

2 tbsp. of olive oil

1 tsp. of paprika

Method:

Rinse off the chick peas under cold water, put in a blender and add the lime, lemon juice, roasted sesame seeds, garlic, chilli and simply blitz until smooth.

Transfer into a bowl, add the paprika and gradually pour in the olive oil. Stir the mix together, cover with cling film and leave to rest for one hour.

Serve and garnish with paprika and a drizzle of olive oil.

Garlic and Aubergine Paste

Ingredients:

2 aubergines, washed and pierced with a fork

5 cloves of garlic, peeled

Juice of 1 lemon

1 tbsp. of chopped parsley

1 tsp. of paprika

3 tbsp. of olive oil

Black pepper

Method:

Bake the aubergines in a preheated oven (180°C, or Gas mark 4) for 20-25 mins until the skin blisters, then remove from the oven and let cool.

When cool, peel and put into a blender with the garlic, lemon juice, paprika and olive oil and blitz until smooth. Season with a pinch of cracked black pepper. Cover and leave in the fridge for an hour before serving and garnish with a sprinkle of parsley.

Tasty Guacamole

Ingredients:

2-3 soft, ripe avocados

1 clove of garlic, finely diced

1 red onion, finely diced

Juice of 1 lime

Method:

Halve and pit the avocados and scoop the flesh out of each avocado using a soup spoon. Into a bowl, add the garlic, lime juice and red onion, mixing all the ingredients together with a fork or potato masher until roughly smooth. Serve with gluten-free tortilla chips or as a side with spicy chicken.

Roasted Sweet Potato and Garlic
(Serves Four)

Ingredients:

1 sweet potato, unpeeled and cut into wedges

1 bulb of garlic, unpeeled cloves

Bunch of fresh basil

1 tbsp. of smoked paprika

3 tbsp. of rapeseed or sunflower oil

Salt and pepper

Method:

Add the oil, smoked paprika, sweet potato, garlic and season in a roasting tray. Stir to ensure they are all well covered before arranging the wedges so they are skin side down. Season with salt and pepper and transfer to a preheated oven (200°C, Gas mark 5) for 30-35 mins until golden brown.

Serve with a garnish of ripped basil leaves.

ROASTED SWEET POTATO AND GARLIC

Prawn Pil Pil
(Serves Two)

Ingredients:

8-10 peeled tiger prawns or langoustine

1 chilli, sliced with seeds

3-4 cloves garlic, sliced

Juice of ½ lemon

1 tsp. of paprika

Dash of white wine

100ml olive oil

Cassoulet dish or any oven proof dish suitable for serving

Fresh parsley

Method

Pop the dish into the preheated oven (180°C, Gas mark 4).

Put olive oil into a cold pan along with lemon juice, paprika, white wine, garlic and chilli. Put on a medium heat and when the oil is infused into ingredients, normally after a couple of minutes, add the prawns.

Simmer for 2-3 minutes, turning halfway through. Remove the dish from the oven and place on a heat-resistant mat and pour the mix into the dish.

Garnish with some freshly chopped parsley and serve in a dish sizzling along with some freshly baked gluten-bread or a nice side salad.

Fennel and Carrot Salad

Ingredients:

2 bulbs of fennel

Juice of 1 lemon

1 carrot, peeled

Salt and pepper

Sprig of parsley

Method:

To prepare the fennel, cut off the top and base of the fennel and grate using the large side of the grate. Add the juice of the lemon as this stops discolouration.

Grate one carrot and mix all ingredients, adding a pinch of the salt and pepper to taste. Add parsley.

This is a great, refreshing salad that goes especially well with fish.

FROZEN LEMON: Always keep a lemon in the freezer. Grate the lemon, rind and all, over any salad for a fantastically fresh zesty kick.

Sweet Chilli Red and Dutch Cabbage Coleslaw

Ingredients:

¼ of a head of red cabbage, thinly sliced

¼ of a head of white dutch cabbage, thinly sliced

1 whole, peeled carrot, grated

4 tbsp. of sweet chili sauce

Juice of ½ lime

Salt and pepper

Method:

With a knife or mandolin, slice the cabbage very thinly and add both cabbages together with the carrot, lime juice and sweet chili sauce. Season with salt and pepper to taste. This is a great salad with spicy dishes and barbequed food.

SWEET CHILLI RED AND DUTCH CABBAGE COLESLAW

Pesto Sauce

(Serves Five to Six)

Ingredients:

1 bunch of fresh basil

200ml olive oil

2 cloves of garlic

1 tsp. of honey

Juice of ½ a lemon

Optional (2 tbsp. of pine nuts, lightly toasted under a grill)

Method:

Put all of the ingredients together and blitz in a hand blender or food processer and you have a fresh pesto for dips or a versatile accompaniment to dishes.

Roasted Beetroot Purée

Ingredients:

4 medium sized beetroots

1 clove of garlic

5-6 coriander leaves

2 tbsp. olive oil

Juice ½ Lemon

Salt and pepper

Method:

Preheat the oven (180°C, Gas mark 4). Wrap your beetroots in tinfoil and bake for 35-40 mins until soft. Remove and let cool before peeling. Add all ingredients into a food processor and blend until smooth. Then pass through a fine sieve and season to taste.

This purée works really well as a dip or indeed with salads and fish.

PESTO SAUCE/ROASTED BEETROT PURÉE

Green Pea Purée

Ingredients:

200g of garden peas (frozen)

3-4 mint leaves

Juice ½ Lemon

1 tsp. dill, chopped

Salt and pepper

Method:

Simply put all ingredients into a food processor and blitz until smooth and season with salt and pepper to taste. To get an even more refined purée pass through a sieve. This purée works exceptionally well with fish dishes.

Salsa Sauce

Ingredients:

1 tin chopped tomatoes

1 red onion, finely diced

Juice of ½ lime

½ a deseed chilli, finely chopped

1 beef tomato, diced

1 tsp. of honey

5-6 coriander leaves, roughly chopped

5-6 basil leaves, chopped

2 cloves of garlic, finely diced

Pinch of salt and pepper

Method:

This is a great accompaniment to fish or chicken dishes and perfect even as a snack with corn nachos.

For best results, leave in the fridge to marinade for more than an hour before serving.

Garam Masala

Ingredients:

1 tbsp. of black peppercorns

1 tbsp. of cardamom seeds

1 tbsp. of coriander seeds

1 tbsp. of cumin seeds

2 inch stick of cinnamon broken up

½ tsp. of cloves

½ tsp. of nutmeg

Method:

Put all of these ingredients into a blender or crush together with a pestle and mortar.

Roasted Red Pepper Sauce

Ingredients:

3 red peppers

½ lemon

Olive oil

Salt and pepper

Method:

Rub 3 peppers with olive oil. There are two ways of doing the peppers – blacken on a pan or pop into a preheated oven (200°C, Gas mark 5) for 15 mins. When black, put in a bowl and cover with clingfilm and leave for 10 mins. This makes it easier to peel the blackened skin. Blitz all the ingredients and pass through a sieve, using a spoon to push the smooth texture through leaving the seeds and skin behind.

Homemade Mayo

Ingredients:

1 tbsp. of white wine vinegar

2 egg yolks

250ml of vegetable oil

2 tsp. of Dijon mustard

Method:

Simply add the vinegar into a clean bowl and whisk in the egg yolks. Next add the mustard and slowly whisk in the vegetable oil, starting with a few drops then adding a spoonful at time until the mayonnaise has emulsified and thickened.

Simple Tomato Sauce

Ingredients:

1 large Spanish onion

2-3 cloves of garlic, finely diced

2 stalks of celery, finely diced

1 bell pepper (optional), finely diced

1 tin chopped tomatoes

Juice of a ½ a lemon

1 tsp. honey

Salt and pepper

½ glass of red wine or chicken stock

3-4 sprigs of basil

2 tbsp. olive oil

Tabasco sauce

Method:

Finely dice the onion, garlic, celery and pepper and add to a pan preheated with 2 tbsp. of olive oil and leave to sweat off for 2-3 minutes. Season with salt and pepper before adding either the wine or chicken stock. Leave to reduce for 4-5 minutes on a simmer. Add the tomatoes, ½ tin of water and the lemon juice along with a tsp. of honey, a dash of tabasco sauce and season with salt and pepper. Tear in the basil and return to heat for about 20 minutes.

Mains

Wild Mushroom and Courgette Pasta
(Serves Four)

Ingredients:

This recipe uses the Simple Tomato Sauce *(See Sauces, page 25)*

400g of gluten-free pasta (100g per person)

1 courgette, finely diced

4-5 mushrooms, porcini or chestnut, quartered

Sprig of thyme

Salt and pepper

Juice of ½ lemon

2 tbsp. of olive oil

Fresh basil

Method:

Add 2 tbsp. of olive oil to a pan and, when slightly warm, add the courgettes and mushrooms. Season with salt and pepper, squeeze in ½ a lemon, a sprig of thyme and sauté for 4-5 mins until gently softened. Add the simple tomato sauce to the pan and leave over a medium heat for 3-4 minutes until heated thoroughly.

Remove the pasta when *al dente* (firm but not hard) and strain before adding to the sauce, ensuring the pasta is totally covered. Garnish with some fresh basil leaves and pepper. Serve in the pan on the table and let people help themselves.

CHEF'S TIP

Put your pasta on first and in the 10 minutes you take to make the rest of the dish, it'll be ready.

Baked Stuffed Peppers served on a Roasted Red Pepper and Tomato Sauce
(Serves Four)

Ingredients:

This requires a Roasted Red Pepper Sauce
(See Sauces page 25)

4 whole peppers, topped and cleaned out

1 carrot, finely diced

400g mushroom, finely diced

400g onion, finely diced

100g celery, finely diced

200g tomato, finely diced

4 slices of beef tomato

125g long grain rice

2 sprigs of dill, finely chopped

2-3 sprigs of parsley, finely chopped

Salt and pepper

1 tbsp. of olive oil

1 litre of vegetable stock

Method:

Boil the rice in vegetable stock for 15 mins, topping up with more stock if required. Meanwhile, put the olive oil onto a pan and, when hot, add all the diced ingredients, dill and parsley, for 3-4 mins before adding the cooked and drained rice and frying for a further 3-4 mins.

Remove from the heat and stuff your peppers to the top, capping with the slice of beef tomato. Place the peppers in a baking or roasting dish, add stock to the dish until the peppers are half submerged and cook in a preheated oven (180°C, Gas mark 4) for 45 mins.

Garnish with celery leaves.

To make the Roasted Red Pepper Sauce
(See Sauces page 25)

Courgette, Sundried Tomato and Rocket Omelette
(Serves Four)

Ingredients:

2 tbsp. of olive oil

2 large courgettes, sliced thinly length ways

1 clove of garlic, diced finely

1 red onion, diced finely

200g of rocket lettuce

100g of sundried tomatoes

16 fresh basil leaves

1 tbsp. of fresh chopped parsley

8 large eggs

Salt and cracked black pepper

1 tsp. lemon juice

Method:

In a large non-stick frying pan, heat 1 tbsp. of olive oil and fry the courgettes until both sides are golden brown before removing. In a large bowl, whisk the eggs and season with a pinch of salt and pepper.

Heat another tbsp. of oil in the same pan and fry the onion and garlic for a minute before adding in the whisked eggs. Gently spread the mix with a fork and leave to cook the base of the omelette for 2-3 mins. Place the omelette under a preheated grill for a couple of minutes until the top is also firm.

Do not fold the omelette. Slide out of pan onto a large plate or platter and add the courgette strips neatly across the top, placing back under the grill for 1-2 mins.

Finally add the sundried tomatoes, rocket, basil, parsley, lemon juice and a pinch of salt and cracked black pepper.

Stuffed Cabbage Leaves in a Tomato and Basil Sauce

(Serves Four)

Ingredients:

1 head of Savoy cabbage, remove leaves and wash

2 tbsp. of vinegar

100g of long grain rice

2 carrots, peeled and diced

3 cloves of garlic, diced

2 mixed bell peppers, diced

2 sticks of celery, diced

3 tomatoes, sliced

100 ml of white wine (optional)

3 tbsp. of olive oil

1 leek, diced

2 red onions, diced

1 courgette, diced

Bunch of flat leaf parsley, roughly chopped

Bunch of basil, roughly chopped

1 bunch of fresh thyme

500 ml of vegetable stock

2 tins of chopped tomatoes

Salt and pepper

Method

Put a large pan on a high heat add 1¼ litres of water and the vinegar, bringing to the boil before adding the cabbage leaves. Blanch for 4-5 mins until soft, remove and cool under cold water and leave aside until later.

Put a deep pan or pot on a med to high heat and add the olive oil. When hot, add in 2 cloves of garlic, red onion, celery, courgette, carrots, leek, peppers and rice and sweat off for 4-5 mins. Add in 3-4 sprigs of thyme and the wine, simmering for another 2-3 mins. Season with salt and pepper and pour in 300ml of vegetable stock. Cook for another 5 mins before removing from heat and leaving to cool.

Place 1 cabbage leaf on a plate and add 1-2 tbsp. of the mix onto the centre of the leaf. Roll into a cone shape and do this with all the leaves and the remaining mix.

When you have all the leaves stuffed put the chopped tomatoes in a large pot with mixed herbs, garlic and the rest of the vegetable stock.

Then place all the stuffed cabbage leaves in a circular pattern into the pot, coating each one with the sauce, add sliced tomatoes and cover the pot and place on a low heat for 35 mins.

Rustic Vegetable and Roasted Almond Bake

Ingredients:

100g of Quinoa, rinse well under cold water

2 tbsp. of olive oil

Salt/pepper

1 tbsp. of honey

1 tbsp. of smoked paprika

1 leek, diced

1 courgette, roughly chopped

2 carrots, peeled and roughly chopped

1 butternut squash, peeled and roughly chopped

1 red onion, roughly chopped

1 aubergine, roughly chopped

3 cloves of garlic

3 sticks of celery, roughly chopped

4-8 mushrooms, cut into quarters

2 mixed bell peppers, roughly chopped

100g of frozen peas

100g of green beans

12 vine cherry tomatoes (leave 6 on the vine to use as a garnish)

2 tins of chopped tomatoes

1 tbsp. of tomato purée

250ml of vegetable stock

25g of sesame seeds

25g of poppy seeds

50g of sliced almonds

Bunch of sage, basil, parsley, roughly chopped

Method:

Preheat oven to 180°C, Gas mark 4. Place a pot or deep pan on a high heat. When hot, add the oil, add in the onion, garlic, carrots, courgette, aubergine, peppers, celery, butternut squash, mushrooms and leek. Season with a pinch of salt, and pepper and cook for 3-4 mins on a high heat to seal in all the flavours.

Lower the heat to medium and add the chopped herbs, quinoa, 6 cherry tomatoes just popped open with your hand, 2 tins of chopped tomatoes, honey, paprika, green beans, peas and vegetable stock, stir well and simmer for 8-10 mins.

Add the tomato purée and place the entire mix in an oven proof dish, sprinkle the seeds and almonds on top of the mix, add the cherry tomatoes still on the vine on top. Drizzle with a little olive oil and cook in oven for 10 mins until the almonds have browned lightly.

Cannelloni Style Beef Crêpe
(Serves Four)

Crêpe ingredients:

1 litre mineral water

350g gluten-free flour

5g baking powder

Pinch of salt and pepper

Dill

Olive oil

Beef Ragu:

500g minced beef

1 medium onion, finely diced

2 carrots, finely diced

3 sticks of celery, finely diced

2 tins of chopped tomatoes

1 tsp. of honey

Pinch of salt and pepper

1 tbsp. of mixed herb

1 tsp. paprika

1 glass of red wine

2 cloves of garlic, finely diced

2 Bay leaves

4 tbsp. of olive oil

Method:

For the crêpe mixture, add the flour, baking powder, mineral water, salt, pepper and dill in a bowl and mix well until all ingredients are thoroughly combined.

For the ragu sauce, pour the olive oil into a large pan or pot and, when hot, add in the garlic, onion, celery and carrots. Cook for 4-5 minutes and then add the wine, salt, pepper, paprika and bay leaves. Leave to simmer for a further 4-5 minutes. Stir in the chopped tomatoes and honey, leaving on a gentle simmer for 15-20 minutes.

For the beef, heat 1 tbsp. of olive oil in a pan and fry the mince, seasoning with salt and pepper. When the beef is nearly cooked, strain and add half the ragu sauce and mixed herbs to the beef. Leave on a gentle simmer for 8 to 10 minutes.

While your beef is simmering, place another medium sized non-stick pan on a high heat to cook your crêpes. Heat 1 tbsp. of olive oil and pour in a small amount of your crêpe mixture into the centre of your pan, moving the pan while doing so to coat the base of the pan, cooking for roughly one minute on each side until lightly brown.

Once the beef is cooked, simply add 2-3 tbsp. of the beef into the crêpe and roll, place on the centre of the plate and pour 2-3 tbsp. of your sauce on top of each crêpe.

CANNELLONI STYLE BEEF CRÊPE

Meatballs
(Serves Four to Six)

Ingredients:

1 kg of beef mince

½ kg of minced pork

2-3 sprigs of fresh basil

2-3 sprigs of parsley

½ courgette, diced

½ bell pepper, diced

1 stick of celery, diced

3 cloves of garlic. diced

Juice of ½ a lime

1 tin chopped tomatoes

1 onion, finely chopped

½ fresh chilli, finely chopped

1 chicken stock cube

½ glass of a good red wine

6 cherry tomatoes

1 tbsp. tabasco sauce

2 tbsp. olive oil

For garnish:

2 gherkins, finely chopped

1 lime

6 cherry tomatoes

Fresh parsley, celery and basil leaves

Method:

Throw all the chopped and diced veg, pork and mince into a large mixing bowl and mix well with a very generous measure of salt and pepper, tbsp. of tabasco sauce and lime.

Break off into meatballs into whatever size you want, as long as they are roughly the same so they cook evenly. Put a non-stick pan on a high heat with 2 tbsp. of olive oil and when bubbling, put the meatballs on. Cook the meatballs for about 5 mins, turning once.

While that is cooking prepare for the ragu sauce by frying off the courgette, garlic, pepper and celery. Take half a dozen cherry tomatoes and squeeze so they break over the pan and some of the tomato juices flow in along with the ½ glass of red wine, reducing the heat to simmer. After the liquid has reduced, add the tin of chopped tomatoes and crumble in a chicken stock cube. Get 2-3 sprigs of basil and roll into a ball before chopping and throwing on top. Cover with another pan or lid and leave it simmer for a further 20-25 minutes.

When finished, garnish with fresh parsley, basil and the leaves from your celery. For an extra kick of flavour add two chopped gherkins with some fresh lime wedges and some cherry tomatoes.

This can be served with meatballs or as a tapas dish on its own. Indeed, you can substitute the beef and pork for minced chicken and cover in sesame seeds.

One Pot Beef Goulash
(Serves Four)

Ingredients:

1 kg of stewing beef

3 tbsp. of rapeseed or sunflower oil

2 peppers, deseed and roughly chopped

6-8 chestnut mushrooms, halved

2 cloves of garlic, roughly sliced

1 large onion, roughly chopped

3 tbsp. of paprika

1 chilli, sliced

1 courgette, roughly chopped

1 tsp. of dried mixed herbs

2 beef stock cubes

1 tbsp. of gluten-free flour

1 tin of chopped tomatoes

Method:

Coat all the beef pieces in well-seasoned flour and fry the meat in a casserole dish or pot that's been preheated with the oil.

Once all the beef is browned, remove from the pot and throw the rest of the ingredients (except the tomatoes) into the pot. Sweat off for 2-3 mins then add in the beef back in along with the paprika. Dilute the stock cubes in 1 litre of boiling water and stir into the pot with the tin of chopped tomatoes.

If using a casserole dish, cover and place in a preheated oven (150°C or Gas mark 3) for 2½ - 3 hours. If using a pot, also cover and leave on a gentle simmer for the same length of time.
Serve with rice or potatoes.

Seared Fillet of Beef with a Mango and Chilli Salsa
(Serves Four)

Ingredients:

4 six ounce fillet steaks, or one whole piece of fillet steak (24 ounces)

2 tbsp. of cracked black pepper

1 tbsp. of rock salt or course sea salt

3 tbsp. of olive oil

1 ripe mango, peeled and finely diced

3 plum tomatoes, finely diced

1 clove of garlic, finely diced

1 chilli, deseeded, and finely diced

Juice of 1 lime

Pinch of salt and pepper

Method:

For the mango and chilli, salsa, simply mix the mango, tomatoes, garlic, chilli and lime juice together with a pinch of salt and pepper.

To sear the beef, place a large pan or griddle pan on a high heat. (If using a griddle pan, rub the olive oil onto the beef, rather than placing into pan and make sure pan is very hot.)

Add in the olive oil and when hot, add in the beef, seasoning with rock salt and cracked black pepper, all the way around the beef.

Cook all sides until golden brown and then sear top and bottom of the beef, this will keep in all of the natural juices and flavours. If you like your beef medium rare, cook on a high heat for 6-8 mins.

Remove the pan from the heat but leave the beef on the pan, allowing to rest for 4-5 mins.

When rested, take a sharp knife to slice your beef into thin slices and serve on a large plate or platter with some crisp salad leaves, dressed with olive oil and lemon juice. Simply, serve your salsa on the side.

This beef is also fantastic when cooked on a barbeque.

Spicy Beef/Lamb Kebabs
(8 skewers, Serves Four)

Ingredients:

800g of minced beef or lamb

1 tbsp. of chili flakes, add more if you like it spicier

2 cloves of garlic, finely chopped

1 medium onion, finely diced

1 tsp. of salt

1 tsp. of pepper

1 tbsp. of paprika

2 sprigs of fresh thyme leaves

2 tbsp. of olive oil

8 wooden skewers

Method:

Add the minced beef or lamb into a bowl with the rest of the ingredients, mixing thoroughly. Take out roughly 100g of the mix per skewer, allowing two per person.

On a wood en skewer, pierce the meat and roll into a sausage shape on flat surface. Place a large pan onto a high heat, put 2 tbsp. of olive oil onto the pan and when hot, add in the kebabs, four at a time, and cook for 6 to 8 minutes, turning periodically. (Can also be cooked on a barbeque).

This dish is great when served with gluten and dairy-free tortillas, Garlic and Aubergine Paste *(see Page 12)*, Salsa Sauce *(see Page 24)* and Sweet Chilli Red and Dutch Cabbage Coleslaw *(see Page 20)*.

For extra flavour, toss some mixed leaves in a bowl with a squeeze of lime juice.

CHEF'S TIP

Steep the wooden skewers in a bowl of water containing the juice of a lemon and crushed rosemary for about 10 mins before use. This will infuse some lemon and herb flavours into the meat and prevents the skewers for burning when cooking.

SPICY BEEF/LAMB KEBABS

Yummy Beef Hot Pot
(Serves Four)

Ingredients:

1kg of diced chuck steak

100g of gluten-free flour, seasoned with a pinch of salt and pepper

1 onion, diced

1 tbsp. of gluten-free Worcestershire sauce

2 carrots, diced

1 clove of garlic, diced

3 sticks of celery, diced

1 litre of hot Beef stock

4-5 sprigs of fresh thyme

2-3 medium potatoes, peeled

1 tbsp. of dairy free butter, melted

1 tbsp. of olive oil

Salt and pepper

Method:

Pre heat your oven to Gas mark 4 or 180°C.

Coat the beef in the seasoned flour, add olive oil to a pan and wait until the oil is hot. Add the floured, diced beef and cook until golden brown. Remove the beef and, in the same pan add all the well seasoned vegetables and cook for 2-3 mins. Next add the beef and half the fresh thyme to the pan and pour in the hot beef stock and Worcestershire Sauce over the vegetables, bringing to the boil for 3-4 mins and stirring regularly.

Divide the mix equally into 4 individual oven proof dishes. Top with thin slices of potato and brush with the melted butter then sprinkle some fresh thyme leaves on top and season with salt and pepper. Cover each hot pot with tin foil that has earlier been brushed with a light coating of olive oil.

Cook in the oven for 1 hour before removing foil and cooking for a further 40 mins.

Spaghetti Bolognese
(Serves Four)

Ingredients:

500g of round steak mince

400g of dried gluten-free spaghetti

200g of smoked streaky rashers, finely diced

2 tins of chopped tomatoes

8 cherry tomatoes

1 onion, finely diced

2 sticks of celery, finely diced

2 carrots, peeled and finely diced

2 cloves of garlic, finely diced

1 beef stock cube

1 tbsp. of tomato purée

1 glass of good red wine (optional)

1 bunch of fresh basil

2 bay leaves

1 tsp. of dried oregano

2 tbsp. olive oil

1 tbsp. of balsamic vinegar

Salt and pepper

Method:

Heat 2 tbsps. of olive oil in a large pan and add the garlic, onion, carrot, celery, streaky rashers and cherry tomatoes for 4-5 mins before stirring in the mince and cooking for another 8-10 mins. Then mix in the red wine, beef stock cube and balsamic vinegar and leave to simmer for 5 mins. Next add the dried oregano, bay leaves, chopped tomatoes, tomato purée, stirring well and leave on a gentle simmer for 30-40 mins.

Season with a pinch of salt and pepper and throw in some roughly torn basil leaves, stir and remove from the heat.

Cook the spaghetti in boiling salted water as directed and, when cooked, strain and mix the spaghetti and Bolognese in a large bowl, garnishing with fresh basil before serving.

Seared Lamb Cutlets with a Tian of Rosemary Scented Quinoa

(Serves Four)

Ingredients:

200g Quinoa

8 large lamb cutlets on the bone, trimmed of fat

1 beef tomato, diced

1 bunch of fresh mint, roughly chopped

3-4 sprigs of fresh rosemary, leaves removed from stem and roughly chopped

1 pint of chicken stock

1 clove of garlic, finely diced

2 shallots, finely diced (or 1 red onion if you don't have shallots)

1 tbsp. of honey

2½ tbsp. of olive/sunflower oil

100g of frozen peas

Juice of ½ lemon

Salt and pepper

What is Quinoa?

Quinoa is known as the 'wonder grain' as it is gluten-free, high in fibre and a complete protein, meaning it has all nine amino acids. It is a great alternative to rice and can be served cold or warm and is suitable for freezing.

Method:

Bring the chicken stock to the boil and add the Quinoa. Rule of thumb is there should be two parts liquid to one part Quinoa so adjust if necessary.

Cover and leave to simmer for 12-15 mins until the stock has absorbed before transferring to a plate and then add 1 tsp. of olive oil and gently mix through with a fork.

In a small bowl, mix the honey, lemon juice, ½ the chopped rosemary and 3-4 chopped mint leaves.

Heat 1 tbsp. of oil in a pan on high and sear the seasoned lamb cutlets on both sides. Brush one side of the cutlets with the honey mix and place in a preheated oven (160°C, Gas mark 5) for 4-5 mins, or longer if you like well done.

Meanwhile, to prepare the Quinoa Tian, get a hot pan and add 1 tbsp. olive oil, garlic, onion, 1 tbsp. of chopped rosemary, peas, tomato, salt and pepper and sauté for 2-3 mins. Then add the cooked Quinoa and mix carefully, removing from heat once warm.

On the centre of a plate use a scone cutter or Tian ring and spoon the mix in, gently pushing down with the back of a dessert spoon.

Remove the ring and you should be left with a neat tian of the quinoa mix.

Remove the lamb cutlets from the oven and leave to rest for 3-4 mins, place two cutlets on each plate garnish with fresh mint leaves and the juices left from the lamb.

Slow Braised Lamb Shanks with Chunky Vegetables

(Serves Four)

Ingredients:

4 lamb shanks, cut around the very top of shank as this allows the meat to fall down during cooking

1 tbsp. of olive

3 carrots, chopped chunky

2 celery sticks, chopped chunky

1 leek, sliced

2 parsnips, chopped chunky

6 cherry tomatoes

6 cloves of garlic, roughly chopped

2 onions, roughly chopped

2 sprigs of rosemary

1 sprig of thyme

1 bay leaf

2 pints of chicken stock

1 glass of white wine

1 tbsp. of rock salt

1 tbsp. of cracked black pepper

Method:

This is a really simple dish with loads of flavour.

In a large hot pan, add the olive oil before placing the lamb shanks two at a time and fry until golden brown all the way round, seasoning as you turn.

In a large deep roasting tray, add all the garlic, tomatoes and vegetables and place the lamb shanks on top before seasoning the whole tray.

Pour in the stock and wine, add the herbs and cover with tin foil. Place in a preheated oven (140°C, or Gas mark 3) for 3-4 hours until the meat is tender and falling away from the top of the bone. Gently remove the lamb from the tray and strain the remaining juices through a sieve into a bowl or jug.

Serve the vegetables on the centre of a plate, rest the lamb shank on top and drizzle some of the juice over the top. Serve with some baby boiled potatoes and garnish with a sprig of fresh rosemary.

SLOW BRAISED LAMB SHANKS WITH CHUNKY VEGETABLES

Leg of Lamb Fresh Herb Steaks with Minted Peas, Tender Stem Broccoli and Butternut Squash Purée (Serves Four)

Ingredients:

4 x 200g leg of lamb steaks

300g of frozen peas

350g of tender stem broccoli

2 tbsp. of olive oil/rapeseed oil

Salt and pepper

250ml of chicken or vegetable stock

1 butternut squash, roughly chopped in cubes and deseeded, no need to peel

1 bunch of fresh sage

1 bunch of fresh rosemary

1 bunch of fresh mint

1 bunch of fresh thyme

Method:

Place a pot on a medium to high heat before adding the stock, butternut squash, a sprig of rosemary and thyme, leaving to simmer for 10-15 mins until the squash Is soft.

While the squash is cooking, place a large pan on a high heat and, when hot, add two of the lamb steaks at a time. Season well on both sides and when one side of the steak is lightly browned turn and add a mix of fresh herbs to the pan. Cook each side of the steak on a medium heat for 2-3 mins then remove and leave to rest on a warm plate. Place some of the herbs and oil on top and cover with tin foil. While resting, cook the other two steaks with the same method and leave to rest.

Remove the butternut squash from the stock, keeping back 1 cup of stock, and blend until smooth before seasoning with salt and pepper.

Add the cup of stock and 6-7 chopped mint leaves to a pan on a high heat and, when it reaches boiling point, add in the tender stem broccoli and peas, cover and cook for 2-3 mins.

To serve, simply put the minted pea and broccoli mix on the centre of a plate and place the lamb steak on top. Drizzle some of the juices from the lamb over the steak and a spoonful of the butternut squash purée on the side.

Garnish:
To garnish the lamb, make some sage crisps. Simply heat 2 tbsp. of oil in a pan. Add 4-6 sage leaves. Fry until crisp. Remove and place onto some kitchen roll.

LEG OF LAMB FRESH HERB STEAKS

Pork Stirfry
(Serves Four)

Ingredients:

400g of thinly sliced pork fillet

3 tbsps. of sunflower oil or coconut oil

2 tbsps. of corn flour

1 red pepper thinly sliced

1 green pepper thinly sliced

4 baby sweetcorn, sliced length ways in half

4 chestnut mushrooms sliced

1 carrot, peeled and sliced into thin strips

1 chilli, sliced thinly

2 cloves of garlic, sliced thinly

1 tbsp. of fresh ginger, diced

3 spring onions, roughly sliced

Juice of 1 lime

4-5 tbsp. of sweet chilli sauce

100 ml of chicken stock

200g of rice noodles

Salt and pepper

Method:

First prepare the rice noodles by bringing a pot of salted water to the boil and adding the noodles. After 5 mins remove from the heat and leave them in the water for 8-10 mins, then cool down under cold water, strain and leave aside.

Put corn flour onto a plate and season with salt and pepper. Add the pork to the corn flour ensuring all the pieces of pork are well coated and shake off any excess flour.

Place a large pan or wok on a high heat and, when hot, add the oil until it is almost smoking before adding the garlic, chilli, ginger. Stir fry for 1 min to release flavours then add the sliced pork and stir fry for 2-3 mins. Add the peppers, baby corn, carrot, mushrooms, the lime juice and half the chicken stock.

Cook for 1-2 min, stirring all the time, then add in the noodles, sweet chilli sauce and the rest of the stock. Mix well and serve when the noodles are hot, garnishing with sliced spring onion and a wedge of fresh lime.

Mexican Pork Wraps with Mixed Bean and Chilli Bean Salsa

(Serves Four)

Ingredients:

For the Mexican Pork Wraps

4-6 gluten-free corn tortilla wraps

2-3 tbsp. of sunflower oil

200g of thinly sliced pork fillet

100g of long grain rice (cooked)

1 chilli, sliced thinly

2 cloves of garlic, sliced thinly

Bunch of fresh coriander, roughly chopped

1 red pepper, sliced thinly

Juice of 1 lime

2 tbsp. of mayonnaise

1 tsp. of chilli powder

Ingredients:

For the salsa

Pinch of salt and pepper

1 tin of sweet corn

1 tin of chilli beans

1 tin of mixed beans

1 clove of garlic, diced

1 chilli, finely diced

1 red onion, finely diced

1 beef tomato, roughly diced

Bunch of coriander, roughly chopped

2 tsp. of honey

Juice of 1 lime

Method:

In a hot pan or wok add the oil, garlic and chilli and cook for 1 min to infuse, then add the pork fillet and cook for a further 2-3 mins. Add the pepper and fry for another 2-3 mins until the pork is cooked through, remove from the heat and mix in some chopped coriander.

Put the mayonnaise in a bowl and mix 1 tsp. of chilli powder and the lime juice.

To serve, spread the chilli mayo evenly over the tortilla and place 2-3 tbsp. of the pork mix and rice into the centre. Sprinkle a few coriander leaves on top and roll. Serve with your home made salsa on the side.

Method:

Simply mix ingredients all together in a bowl. Cover and leave aside or in your fridge for an hour or so to let all the flavours infuse!

This is a very simple salsa that is also a great accompaniment for chicken and prawns.

Crispy Pork Cutlet with Braised Sultana, Apple, Red Cabbage and Sweet Onion Cider Sauce (Serves Four)

Ingredients:

4 x 220g pork cutlets with rind on

3 tbsp. of rapeseed or sunflower oil

Salt and pepper

½ head red cabbage, thinly sliced or shredded

50g of sultanas

2 eating apples, cored and diced skin on

Juice of 1 lemon

2 tbsp. of brown sugar

2 tbsp. of white wine vinegar

3 medium sized onions, peeled and sliced

1 bunch of fresh sage

250ml of chicken/ vegetable stock

1 x 330ml bottle of cider

Method:

Make sure the skin on the pork cutlets is dry and rub salt and pepper into it. Put a large pan on a medium heat, add the oil and place the cutlets on their edge skin side in the oil. Cook for 10-12 mins until the skin is brown and crispy, then cook on either side for 4-5 mins. Remove from the pan, place on a warm plate and leave to rest.

Turn up the pan to a high heat. Throw in 6-8 sage leaves and cook for 1-2 mins until crispy. Remove and place on kitchen paper. These are really tasty and make a great garnish.

Using the same pan, add in the onion and cider and season with salt and pepper. Cook until the cider has reduced and has made the onions wonderfully sweet.

While the pork is cooking, place a pot on a medium heat and add half the stock, sultanas, red cabbage, white wine vinegar and brown sugar. Leave to simmer and stir well until the liquid has reduced by half, then add the rest of the stock and cook until reduced.

When the cabbage is just *al dente*, mix in the apple and lemon juice and remove from the heat, covering with a lid until required.

To serve, place a good helping of the red cabbage on the centre of plate, place the cutlet on top and garnish with the crispy sage leaves and the sweet onion sauce on the side.

Coconut Chicken Curry
(Serves Four)

Ingredients:

4 skinless chicken fillets, cut into rough cubes

300g basmati rice

2 bay leaves

1 tbsp. of sunflower or coconut oil

1 bell pepper, diced

1 large onion, peeled and finely diced

1 knob of fresh ginger, peeled and finely chopped

2 cloves of garlic, peeled and finely chopped

1 bunch of coriander

2 spring onions, thinly sliced

200ml of hot chicken stock

100ml of coconut milk, full fat

1 tsp. of garam masala

You can buy Garam Masala but just make sure it is gluten-free or you can make your own as it will last for months in an air tight jar. *(see page 24)*

Method:

Half fill a medium size pot with salted water and bring to the boil. Add the bay leaves and rice and cook for 10 minutes until the rice is tender. Drain well and leave to one side.

Meanwhile heat the oil in a large frying pan. Add in the garlic, onion, ginger, pepper and fry for 2 mins. Add the chicken and 1 tsp. of garam masala, cooking for a further 3-4 mins until all the chicken has been sealed.

Pour over the hot chicken stock and turn the heat down to a simmer for a 6-8 mins until the chicken is cooked through. Stir in the coconut milk gently, let simmer for another 2mins.

Serve on a bed of rice and garnish with fresh sprigs of coriander and spring onion.

Spatchcock Chicken with Summer Salad
(Serves Four)

Ingredients:

1 large chicken

5 cloves fresh garlic, whole

Ginger, 1 cm roughly chopped

Sprig of thyme, torn

1 red chilli, finely chopped

Juice of 1 lemon

1 tbsp. of paprika

1 tbsp. of Cajun seasoning

Olive oil

Salt and pepper

Ingredients:
Zesty Summer Salad

Mango, avocado and lemon-zested leaves

Mixed salad leaves

2 small cooked beetroots, chopped

1 avocado, chopped

10-12 cherry tomatoes, halved (or sundried tomatoes)

1 mango, peeled and chopped

½ cucumber, chopped

½ lemon

Fresh basil leaves

2 tbsp. olive oil

Method:

Preheat oven to 200°C, Gas mark 4.

Spatchcock is simply the name given to a way that chicken is cut so that it is essentially a single flat piece of meat.

Score chicken along the breast and thighs, rubbing in the olive oil, paprika and cajun seasoning, ensuring the chicken is well covered, before drizzling the lemon juice over it.

Preheat a large pan or roasting tray for 2 mins before adding 3 tbsp. of olive oil and placing the chicken with the skin side facing down. Add the ginger, garlic and chilli before turning the heat down to medium and leaving for 4-5 minutes to seal. Turn chicken and add thyme, cooking for another 4-5 minutes until golden brown before popping into the preheated oven for 25 mins.

Once the chicken is cooked, serve on a zesty summer salad. My favourite is to get a platter and cover with any mixed salad leaves, chunks of cucumber, juice of ½ lemon and roughly chopped cooked beetroot. Peel a ripe mango and avocado and thinly slice before scattering over salad. Garnish with fresh basil leaves, cherry or sundried tomatoes and drizzle with olive oil.

Cut chicken into serving-sized portions and place on top of the salad. This dish is great for BBQs.

Spicy Chicken Penne Paprika
(Serves Four)

Ingredients:

3 skinless chicken fillets, sliced into thin strips

1 onion, finely chopped

2 cloves of garlic, finely chopped

2 chilli peppers, sliced thinly with seeds left in

1 tin of chopped tomatoes

600ml or 1 pint of chicken stock (add 1 chicken stock cube to 1 pint of boiling water)

½ tbsp. of paprika

1 tsp. of honey

2 mixed bell peppers, roughly sliced

1 tbsp. of chopped parsley

Juice of ½ lemon

400g of gluten-free penne pasta

Parsley and basil leaves for garnish

Black pepper

Method:

In a deep pan or wok, bring the chicken stock to the boil and add the sliced chicken, seasoning with a pinch of black pepper. Leave it for 6 mins ensuring all the chicken is coated with the liquid.

Add the lemon juice, garlic, chilli, peppers, onion and paprika and cook for a further 3-4 mins, so all the flavours are well infused. Stir in the chopped tomatoes and honey, leaving to simmer on a low heat for 6-8 mins.

Meanwhile cook the pasta in boiling salted water. When the pasta is cooked and strained, gently mix in the chicken and serve in a large bowl, garnishing with chopped parsley and fresh basil leaves.

STOCK: Never throw away your stock. Get a deep muffin tray and fill it all before freezing. Transfer to freezer bags and, depending on tray, two will usually equal 1 cup of stock for most recipes.

Courgette Stuffed with Chicken and Mixed Vegetables in a Ragu Sauce

(Serves Four)

Ingredients:

4 chicken breasts, minced

6 courgettes

1 large onion, finely diced

200gm mushroom, finely diced

1 whole bell pepper, finely diced

A bunch of parsley, finely chopped

Salt and pepper

1 tbsp. of olive oil

1 pint of chicken stock

Method:

To prepare the courgettes for stuffing, slice them into roughly 6 cm pieces. With a teaspoon, remove the core of the courgette so you have a hollow tube affect.

To make the stuffing, put the chicken through a mincer, or get your butcher to do this for you. Place the chicken in a bowl and thoroughly mix with all the other finely diced ingredients along with a tbsp. of olive oil and season with salt and pepper.

With a teaspoon, fill your courgette pieces with the stuffing. When all your courgettes are filled, in a deep roasting or baking tray, add one pint of chicken stock and place the stuffed courgettes standing vertically and put into a preheated oven (180°C or Gas mark 4) for 40-45 minutes.

Ingredients:
Ragu sauce

1 tin of chopped tomatoes

1 onion, finely diced

1 stick of celery, finely diced

1 tsp. of honey

Method:

Place all in a pot and bring to a simmer for 8-10 mins.

When the stuffed courgettes are ready, add 2-3 tbsp. of the juice from the tray to the tomato sauce.

Pour some sauce in a bowl and place the courgettes on top and serve.

Rustic Roast Chicken Legs and Thighs with Lemon and Ginger Rice
(Serves Four)

Ingredients for Chicken:

4 chicken thighs and 4 chicken drumsticks

1 chilli, sliced

Juice of 2 limes

Fresh ginger, peeled and sliced into 1 cm cubes

2 cloves of fresh garlic, roughly sliced

Salt and pepper

2 tsp. of smoked paprika

2 tsp. of tabasco

1 tbsp. of honey

3 tbsp. of olive oil

Garnish of celery leaves, 2 sprigs of coriander, slices of lemon

Ingredients for Lemon and Ginger Rice:

400g rice

3 lemons, 2 juiced and zest of 1

Ginger, cubed to the size of two cloves of garlic

3-4 medium sized mushrooms, diced

Sprig of thyme

1 clove of garlic, diced

1 red pepper, diced

1 medium sized red onion, diced

A fistful of frozen peas

1 tin of sweetcorn

A small bunch of green beans, topped and tailed

Coriander

Method:

Lightly score the chicken to allow flavours infuse into the meat. Place all the ingredients into a casserole dish and mix thoroughly by hand to ensure the chicken is thoroughly coated. Cover with a lid or tin foil and leave to marinade for an hour.

Place into preheated oven (180°C, Gas mark 4) and leave for 40 to 50 mins depending on the size of the chicken pieces. This dish is ideal for both BBQ and as a main served with lemon rice (See recipe for Lemon and Ginger Rice below).

Serving Suggestion:

When cooked, serve on a large platter with lemon slices, celery leaves and coriander.

Method:

Boil the rice with the juice of one lemon and ½ the ginger.

When rice is cooked, remove and run under the cold water tap for a minute as it helps keep the rice nice and fluffy. Return to the heat along with the juice of one lemon and all the diced ingredients along with the frozen peas and sweetcorn. Soften for about 2 minutes.

Put all the ingredients into a serving bowl and mix with the juice of a squeezed lemon.

Garnish with a couple of sprigs of coriander and wedges of lemon.

Sesame and Poppy Seed Garlic Chicken Balls

(Serves Four)

Ingredients:

2 chicken fillets or 400g of chicken, roughly chopped

4 cloves of garlic, roughly chopped

4 spring onions, sliced

1 tbsp. of parsley, chopped

1 tbsp. of fresh dill, chopped

Pinch of salt and pepper

1 egg

3 tbsp. of sesame seeds

1 tbsp. of poppy seeds

Oil for deep frying

Method:

Using a food processor, blend the chicken, garlic and spring onion together until a smooth texture.

Transfer to a bowl and add the egg, salt, pepper and chopped herbs, mixing all ingredients together.

Place the sesame and poppy seeds on a plate, shape the chicken mix into balls roughly 30g each and coat with the seeds.

Deep fry in hot oil for 3-4 mins until golden brown and then place in a preheated oven (180°C, Gas mark 4) for 8 mins. Serve with salad and a homemade garlic mayonnaise.

Garlic Mayonnaise

Into a blender, add 2 cloves of garlic
2 sprigs of fresh parsley
4 tbsp. of mayonnaise

Blend until smooth and serve.

Chicken and Lemongrass Skewers with Spicy Crispy Oriental Salad

(Serves Four)

Ingredients:

For the Chicken and Lemongrass Skewers

6 x 170g chicken fillet, cubed

8 x lemongrass

1 bunch of fresh thyme

2 tbsp. of honey

Juice of 1 lemon

4 tbsp. of olive oil

Salt and pepper

Method:

In a bowl, mix the cubed chicken, honey, some fresh thyme leaves and lemon juice with a pinch of salt and pepper before popping into the fridge to marinate for 5-10 mins.

When infused, cut an angle at the end of the lemon grass so it makes it easier to skewer the chicken. Heat the oil in a pan on a medium to high heat, then fry the chicken skewers on each side until thoroughly cooked through.

Garnish with fresh thyme and use some of the oil left in the pan to drizzle over the chicken.

Ingredients:

For the Spicey Crispy Oriental Salad

100g of sugar snaps, sliced

100g of bean sprouts

8 baby sweet corn, sliced

2 chillies, sliced leaving seeds in

Juice of 2 limes

1 tbsp. of grated ginger

2 cloves of garlic, thinly sliced

50g of mixed bean sprout seeds

Bunch of coriander, roughly chopped

2 tbsp. of sesame oil

1 tsp. of honey

Method:

Mix the honey, sesame oil and lime juice together.

Mix all the other ingredients together in a bowl and add the sauce, tossing together gently.

Seared Monkfish and Scallops with Fennel and Roasted Red Pepper Sauce
(Serves Four)

Ingredients:

800g monkfish, or two full monkfish fillets

8 scallops

1 tbsp. capers

1 bulb of fennel, thinly sliced

2 tbsp. gluten-free flour

Salt and pepper

6 tbsp. olive oil

Splash of white wine

250ml chicken or vegetable stock

Roasted Red Pepper Sauce *(See sauces page 25)*

1 lemon

Dill

Method:

Firstly, prepare the Roasted Red Pepper Sauce *(See Sauces page 25)*.

Season the flour with salt and pepper and scatter on a flat surface. Lightly dust the monkfish on both sides and tap to remove excess flour and put aside on a plate. Heat the olive oil in a pan on medium heat, add monkfish for about 2-4 mins until it is lightly browned before popping into a preheated oven (180°C, Gas mark 4) for 8-10 mins.

While monkfish is in the oven, prepare the scallops by removing the muscle and scoring the scallops with an X, thus helping them cook more evenly. Depending on individual taste, you can remove the orange coral part. Season with salt and pepper.

Put 250ml of chicken or vegetable stock into the pan along with juice of half a lemon, the fennel, capers and the white wine. Simmer for 4-6 mins, until the fennel is *al dente*. When cooked, strain off any excess juice, cover and leave to one side.

Next, remove monkfish from oven and leave to rest in the pan for 3-4 mins.

Put a second non-stick pan on a high heat and when it begins to smoke, add 2 tbsp. of olive oil and then add the scallops, scored side down first, cooking for approx. 1-2 mins on each side until golden brown.

Add the Roasted Red Pepper Sauce to a pan and simmer on a low heat.

In the centre of a plate, spread 2–3 tbsp. of the Roasted Red Pepper Sauce before adding 2-3 tbsp. of the fennel mix. Slice the monkfish in half and serve on top of the fennel along with the scallops and coral, garnishing with a wedge of fresh lemon and dill.

Steamed Mussels in Fresh Ginger, Lime and Garlic Broth

(Serves Two, or Four as a starter)

Ingredients:

1 kg of organic Irish mussels

1 lime

2-3 sprigs of dill

1 sprig of coriander

2 sticks of celery, diced

2 cloves of garlic, crushed

Fresh ginger (size of 1 garlic clove), finely chopped

½ medium onion, finely diced

6 cherry tomatoes

½ ltr vegetable or chicken stock

Salt and black pepper

Coriander, dill, basil and lime for garnish

Method:

Boil the stock in a large pot before squeezing in the juice of half a lime. Reduce to a medium heat and add the diced celery, ginger, garlic and onion.

Roughly chop the coriander and dill and add to the pot along with a pinch of black pepper, leaving it for 2-3 minutes so the flavours can infuse.

Add the mussels and cover pot, leaving to steam for a further 2-3 minutes until all the mussels have opened. Discard any mussels that haven't opened as they may be bad.

In the meantime, cut the cherry tomatoes into quarters and sprinkle with black pepper.

Serve the mussels in a deep dish or bowl and garnish with the cherry tomatoes, wedges of lime, a couple of sprigs of dill and some freshly torn basil. If having it for brunch, it is great served with a homemade gluten-free bread.

CHEF'S TIP

This is a simple, quick and versatile dish that can be served up as a starter or, by doubling the quantities, provide a more filling brunch.

STEAMED MUSSELS IN FRESH GINGER, LIME AND GARLIC BROTH

Zesty Crab Claws with Avocado Salad
(Serves Four)

Ingredients:

6–8 crab claws per person, cooked and shelled. If using fresh crab claws boil in salty water for 10 mins. remove, let cool and shell.

2 limes juiced & zest of 1 lime – grate the skin of 1 lime on a cheese grater

2 cloves of garlic, sliced thinly

1 bunch of flat leaf parsley, roughly chopped

2 ripe avocados

8 cherry tomatoes, quartered

2 heads of baby gem lettuce

100ml of olive oil

Pinch of salt and pepper

Method:

Pour the olive oil into a cold large pan and add the garlic and lime juice and bring to a gentle simmer. Mix the cooked crab claws and lime zest together, cooking for 6-8 mins until the claws are warm and completely coated in the oil.

While the crab claws are warming and flavours infusing, get a large plate or platter and scatter washed baby gem leaves around the plate. Peel the avocados. Remove the stones and cut into rough chunks.

Remove the crab claws from the pan and place on the plate, and then pour all the juices from the pan over the claws and lettuce.

Garnish with the chunks of avocado, cherry tomatoes and roughly chopped flat leaf parsley. Season the whole dish with a pinch of salt and pepper.

Tempura Tiger Prawns with Cajun Mayo and Oriental Salad

(Serves Four)

Ingredients:
For the Oriental Salad

1 carrot, peeled, cut in half and finely sliced

2 spring onions, finely sliced

2 sticks of celery, cut in half and finely sliced

1 inch of leek, finely sliced

1 tbsp. of sesame oil

Ingredients:
For the Tempura Batter:

12g of gluten-free flour

¼ litre/8.45 fluid ounces of sparkling water, must be cold

1 tsbp of white vinegar

Pinch of salt and pepper

Juice of ½ lemon

Ingredients:
For the Cajun Mayonnaise:

1 tbsp. Cajun seasoning

Juice of ½ lime

4 tbsp. mayonnaise *(See Sauces page 25)*

Ingredients:
For the Tempura Prawns:

20 peeled tiger prawns (5 per portion)

Rapeseed or sunflower oil

Method:

Add the flour into a bowl with the rest of the batter ingredients and whisk roughly. Don't worry if there are any lumps in the batter, just place into the fridge until required.

For the salad, add the carrot, leek, celery and spring onions into a bowl and dress with the sesame oil.

For the cajun mayonnaise, add 4 tbsp. of mayonnaise, 1 tbsp. of cajun seasoning, juice of ½ lime and mix well.

To make the tempura prawns, preheat a deep fryer to 180°C or shallow fry in a wok filling half of the wok with rapeseed or sunflower oil. Lightly dust the prawns in some gluten-free flour and dip into the tempura batter mix and shallow fry for 6-8 minutes. Depending on the size of your pan or fryer, cook 5-10 prawns at a time.

Serve on a large plate with the oriental salad and cajun dip.

Garnish with lemon wedges.

Rustic Fish Casserole
(Serves Four)

Ingredients

400g of mixed fish fillets such as hake, cod, red mullet and salmon but you can add any fish. Just ensure the fish is scaled, pin boned and cut into half.

4 large shell-on king prawns or chopped up lobster if you want to push the boat out

400g of fresh mixed mussels and clams

1 tbsp. of capers

3 sticks of celery, roughly chopped

1 bulb of fennel, roughly chopped

1 butternut squash, using the neck of the squash only, peel and cut into small rough chunks

1 small onion, peeled and diced

2 cloves of garlic, peeled and sliced thinly

1 leek, sliced

1 fresh chilli, sliced

1 tin of chopped tomatoes

1 chicken or vegetable stock cube

1 glass of white wine or 125ml

1 small bunch of fresh basil

1 small bunch of flat leaf parsley

2 tbsp. of olive or sunflower oil

1 tbsp. honey

½ lemon

Pepper

Method:

In a large pot, heat the oil on a high heat, add in all the vegetables, fennel and dill and sweat off for 5-6 mins, stirring constantly.

Stir in the stock cube, add the tin of chopped tomatoes, a glass of water and the wine. Leave to simmer for 10 mins.

Add the honey, fresh basil and parsley, stirring gently.

Place the fillets of fish around the pot skin side up, then place the shell fish neatly around the pot.

Season with a squeeze of lemon juice and pepper and cover with a lid of tin foil and leave to simmer gently on a medium heat until the mussels and clams open.

Garnish with fresh basil parsley and capers.

Dublin Bay Prawns and Smoked Salmon Cocktail

(Serves Four)

Ingredients:

2 slices of smoked salmon, cut into thin strips

1 kg of fresh Dublin Bay prawns

1 tsp. of tabasco

1 tsp. of Worcestershire sauce

1 tbsp. of horseradish

1 tsp. of brandy

2 tbsp. of tomato ketchup

2 heads of baby gem lettuce, washed and roughly sliced

2 tbsp. of paprika

2 gherkins, finely diced

1 lemon, cut into wedges

5 tbsp. mayonnaise, you can use an off the shelf brand or the homemade version if you have time (See Sauces page 25)

Method:

Bring a large pot of salted water to the boil and cook the Dublin Bay prawns and juice of ½ lemon for 2-3 mins. Strain and leave to one side to cool before peeling them.

Put the mayonnaise in a bowl and stir in the ketchup, Worcestershire, tabasco, horseradish, and brandy, seasoning to taste.

To serve:

In a cocktail glass put a tsp. of sauce in the base then the lettuce, smoked salmon and Dublin Bay prawns.

Spoon the cocktail sauce over the top and garnish with the diced gherkins, a pinch of paprika and a wedge of lemon.

CHEF'S TIP

LEMON: To get more juice out of lemon make sure you roll it firmly on a hard surface first as this will break the segments before using.

Seafood Paella
(Serves Four)

Ingredients:

300g of mussels

200g of fresh hake, cut into cubes

200g of fresh salmon, cut into cubes

100g of smoked cod or haddock, cut into cubes

8 tiger prawns

4 scallops, sliced in half (optional)

50 ml olive oil

125g gluten-free chorizo sausage, diced

2 peppers mixed, deseeded and diced

4 cloves of garlic, diced

1 onion, diced

6 cherry tomatoes

100g of frozen peas

1 tsp. of fresh chopped dill

Juice of 1 lemon

Salt and pepper

250g of long grain rice

450ml of chicken or fish stock

1 tbsp. of turmeric or 1 tsp. of saffron strands

Method:

Place a large pan on a high heat and, when hot, add in the chorizo for 2-3 mins to release the sausage oil and then add the onion, garlic, peppers and half the olive oil.

Cook for a further 2-3 mins before mixing in the rice, turmeric, mussels and prawns.

Pop open the cherry tomatoes by squeezing gently so some of the juices run into the dish. Add half the stock and leave to simmer until it has reduced so you have half the liquid left.

Then add the remaining fish, apart from the scallops.

Add the dill, lemon juice, peas and the rest of the stock and leave to simmer until all the liquid is nearly reduced.

Just before you remove from the heat, place the scallops around the top, pushing them in to just cover them.

Leave in for 2-3 mins before serving.

Add salt and pepper to serve.

Fresh Lemon Scented Cod with a Rhubarb Compoté

(Serves Four)

Ingredients:

175g of fresh cod (per serving)

3 sticks of rhubarb, peeled and cut into rough chunks

Juice of ½ lemon

3 tsp. of olive oil

1 tbsp. of honey

A few sprigs of fresh dill

Salt and pepper

50g of gluten-free flour

1 small bunch of cherry tomatoes on the vine

Method:

Put the flour on a plate and season with a pinch of salt and pepper, grate the zest of ½ lemon into the flour (simply using the smallest size on your grater, grate the lemon skin).

Roll the pieces of cod into the flour and coat fully, making sure to tap off any excess flour.

Put a pan on a medium heat and add 2 tbsp. of olive oil.

When the pan is hot add the cod, skin side down and cook for 3-4 mins to get the skin to a nice brown crisp. Turn the fish, add in the cherry tomatoes and cook for a further 4-5 mins.

Remove from the heat, leave to rest in the pan while you finish the rest of the dish.

Put on another pan or small pot on a high heat and add the rhubarb, honey, lemon juice and 3 tbsp. of water. When the rhubarb is soft remove from pan and serve on the side of the plate.

Garnish with the cherry tomatoes, fresh lemon and dill.

Desserts / Cocktails

Dark Chocolate Coconut Slices
(Serves Four)

Ingredients:

To make the Dark Chocolate Slices

3 eggs

3 tbsp. of vegetable oil

90g of castor sugar

100g of gluten-free flour

1 tsp. of gluten-free baking powder

100g of raisins

1 measure of brandy

Icing sugar

Method:

Preheat the oven to 180°C, Gas mark 4.

Put the bandy, raisins and 100ml of boiling water in a pot and leave for 10 mins.

Separate the eggs, whites into a clean mixing bowl and yolks into another bowl.

Mix the egg whites in the blender until stiff and add the sugar, continuing to whisk until the egg whites look like meringue and leave to one side.

Mix the egg yolks with the vegetable oil, flour and baking powder for 8-10 mins until smooth.

Slowly mix all the contents from the two bowls together with a wooden spoon or spatula until fully blended and then add the raisins.

Place lightly into a cake tin or bread tin and cook in oven for 25-30 mins.

To garnish: dust with icing sugar.

Ingredients:

To make the Coconut Dip

100g of dairy-free margarine

150g of castor sugar

4 tbsp. of cocoa powder

4 tbsp. of water

150g of coconut flakes

Method:

Place a pot on a medium heat and add the margarine, castor sugar, cocoa powder and water. Bring to a simmer and continually mix until smooth.

Cut the cake into small squares and dip quickly into the cocoa mix and then into the coconut flakes.

Leave to set and serve.

Brandy Raisin Tea Cake

(Serves Six)

Ingredients:

3 eggs

3 tbsp. of vegetable oil

90g of castor sugar

100g of gluten-free flour

1 tsp. of gluten-free baking powder

100g of raisins

1 measure of brandy

Method:

Preheat the oven to 180°C or Gas mark 4.

Put the bandy, raisins and 100ml of boiling water in a pot and leave for 10 mins.

Separate the eggs, whites into a clean mixing bowl and yolks into another bowl.

Mix the egg whites in the blender until stiff and add the sugar, continuing to whisk until the egg whites look like meringue and leave to one side.

Mix the egg yolks with the vegetable oil, flour and baking powder for 8-10 mins until smooth.

Slowly mix all the contents from the two bowls together with a wooden spoon or spatula until fully blended and then add the soaked raisins.

Place lightly into a cake tin or bread tin and cook in oven for 25-30 mins.

To garnish dust with icing sugar.

Cherry Vanilla Sponge
(Serves Four to Six)

Ingredients:

500ml tin of pitted cherries or 200g of fresh cherries deseeded

4 large eggs

4 tbsp. of vegetable oil

1 tbsp. of cold water

4 tbsp. of castor sugar

½ tsp. of gluten-free baking powder

4 heaped tbsp. of gluten-free flour

1 vanilla pod (cut the pod horizontally and with the tip of your knife scrape out the vanilla)

To make use of the pod, mix it with some sugar and store in an airtight jar.

Baking tin size 24 cm long 14 cm wide 7 cm deep

Method:

Preheat the oven to 180°C, Gas mark 4.

Separate the eggs and put the white of the egg into a clean mixing bowl and whisk for 3-4 mins until semi stiff. While still whisking, add 1 tbsp. of sugar at a time and stir briskly until stiff like meringue and place into another bowl until later.

Wash out your mixing bowl and add the egg yolks with the oil, cold water, flour, vanilla and baking powder, mixing on a medium to high speed for 4-5 mins until stiff.

Blend the two mixes together slowly in a large bowl using a wooden spoon or spatula until they reach a smooth creamy texture.

Brush the tin very lightly with oil and fill with the half the mixture, then add your cherries before topping with the rest of the mixture.

Place in the oven for 25-30 mins. To check if it is cooked, simply push a cocktail stick or skewer into the centre sponge and if it comes out dry it is cooked.

Remove from oven and let cool before dusting with icing sugar.

CHERRY VANILLA SPONGE

Apple and Cinnamon Pie
(Serves Five to Six)

Ingredients:
For the Apple Filling

8 large eating apples (I use Granny Smiths), peeled, cored and roughly chopped

½ tsp. of cinnamon

5 tbsp. of castor sugar

Ingredients:
For the Base

Round cake tin with removable base 26cm diameter and 6cm deep

5 eggs

200g gluten-free flour

150g castor sugar

5 tbsp. of vegetable oil

½ tsp. gluten-free baking powder

1 tbsp. of cold water

Ingredients:
For the Topping

50g of soy margarine

30g castor sugar

120g gluten-free flour

Method:

Simply place the chopped apples in a pot and add the cinnamon and sugar.

Cover with a little greaseproof paper and cook on a low heat for 10-12 mins until the mix is soft. Remove from the heat and leave to cool.

Method:

Preheat oven 180°C, Gas mark 4.
Separate the eggs into two bowls, whites in one and the yolks in another.

Add the egg whites into a mixer and whisk until semi-stiff and while still mixing add the sugar 1 tbsp. at a time until like meringue.

Remove from the mixer and add the yolk to the whites and mix gently together with a wooden spoon or spatula.

Mix in the flour and baking powder, stirring slowly until all ingredients are fully mixed together before finally mixing in the oil.

Very lightly, brush the cake tin with oil and transfer the mix into the tin.

Cook in a preheated oven for 25 mins.

While the base is in the oven prepare the topping.

Method:

Mix all the ingredients in a bowl with your hands and mould into a ball. Put into the fridge for 5-10 mins to set.

Remove the base from the oven and, when cooled in tin, put the apple filling on top.

Using a cheese grater, roughly grate the topping mix over the apple and, when completely covered, place back into the oven for 10-15 mins until lightly golden in colour. Serve warm with a dairy-free ice cream.

APPLE AND CINNAMON PIE

Chocolate Cake with Warm Mixed Berry Compoté

(Serves Four to Six)

Ingredients:
For the Chocolate Sauce

5 eggs

7 tbsp. of castor sugar

6 tbsp. of gluten-free flour

5 tbsp. of vegetable oil

4 tbsp. cocoa powder

Method:
Preheat oven to 180°C, Gas mark 4.

Separate the egg whites and yolks into 2 mixing bowls.

Whisk the egg whites in a mixer until stiff, then add the castor sugar and resume whisking until stiff like meringue.

Remove from mixer and use a wooden spoon or spatula to slowly churn in the flour. When completely blended, slowly add the egg yolks before adding the water and oil.

Gently stir in the cocoa powder until the smooth and then place in a lightly oiled cake tin and cook in the oven for 25-30 mins.

Ingredients:
For the Berry Compoté

100g of strawberries

100g of raspberries

100g of blueberries

4 tbsp. of castor sugar

4 tbsp. of water

Method:
Place all together in a pot and simmer for 3-4 mins.

To serve, let the cake cool add the warm berry compoté on top and serve with a dairy-free ice cream.

Banana and Blueberry Pancakes with Raspberry and Blueberry Compoté

(Serves Four)

Ingredients:
For the Pancakes

2 bananas

4 eggs

50g of blueberries

Olive oil

Method:
Add all the ingredients into a food blender and mix until you get a smooth consistency for your batter. Place a non-stick pan on a med heat and when hot add 1 tsp. of oil, making sure the centre of the pan is coated.

When the oil is hot, add 2-3 tbsp. of the mix onto the centre of the pan and cook for approximately 2-3 mins until each side until golden brown.

Serve with a good helping of Berry Compoté on top.

Ingredients:
For the Berry Compoté

100g of fresh blueberries

100g of fresh raspberries

1 tbsp. of castor sugar

3 tbsp. of water

Method:
Put all the ingredients in a pot and place on a medium heat, stirring very gently until warm and slightly broken down.

Remove from heat and serve on top of your pancakes.

Pre-Dinner

Vodka Punch

In a tall glass, pour over ice, 1 measure of vodka and a ½ measure of blue curacao, add a dash of blackcurrant cordial and top up with 7UP.

Garnish with a lemon wheel.

Gin and Cucumber

In an old fashioned glass put 8 mint leaves, 3 slices of cucumber, juice of one lime and 2 tsp. of sugar, muddle* ingredients to release flavour, add 1 measure of gin and serve over ice.

Garnish with a mint sprig.

Crush using the end of a rolling pin or bartender's muddler if available.

After Dinner

Black Mojito

In an old fashioned glass, add 6 mint leaves, 4 lime wedges, 2 tsp. of sugar, 1 measure of tequila and ¾ measure of crème de cassis, muddle these ingredients to release flavours.

Fill the glass with crushed ice and top up with soda water.

Garnish with a mint sprig.

Basil Daiquiri

To blender, add 10 fresh basil leaves, juice of ½ a lemon, 3 tsp. of sugar and 6-8 ice cubes, into a blender.

Blend well with a measure of white rum and serve in a stemmed cocktail glass.

Garnish with a basil leaf.

VODKA PUNCH

GIN AND CUCUMBER

BLACK MOJITO

BASIL DAIQUIRI

Erika Doolan is one of Ireland's leading nutritional consultants and provides an invaluable service, helping people overcome a range of issues, such as weight and depression, through food and lifestyle changes. She is highly regarded in the food industry and, in addition to providing chefs with nutritional information, is responsible for designing menus for some of the country's best restaurants.

For further information, visit

http://www.erikadoolan.com/

Nutritional Information

Ingredient	Nutrional Information
Sweet Potato	A delicious and filling diet food, orange fleshed sweet potatoes are much lower on the glycemic index than ordinary white potatoes. High in fibre, sweet potatoes help promote digestion. They contain the three main antioxidant vitamins, beta carotene (which is converted by the body into vitamin A) and vitamins C and E. They are also very energising, especially when eaten with protein and they help to eliminate water retention too. Sweet potatoes are the highest low-fat source of Vitamin E, which is essential for healthy skin.
Fennel	Fennel is an excellent source of vitamin C and very good dietary fibre. Fennel is a mild appetite suppressant and is used to improve the kidneys, liver and lungs. Fennel tea also aids digestion.
Beef	Lean beef helps you to lose weight rapidly by raising your metabolism while simultaneously curbing your hunger. It is packed with B vitmains and zinc, excellent for aiding mental health.
Paprika	This delicious spice is extremely high in vitamin C. A whole paprika pepper is known to have six to nine times the amount of vitamin C as a tomato. Because of its high vitamin C content, paprika may also help you absorb iron-rich foods and may help your body fight common infections.
Red Pepper	Slow down or reverse the signs of aging with delicious peppers. This versatile vegetable provides an amazing array of nutrients, including two antioxidants that work well together, vitamin C and beta carotene. Together, these offer protection against cell-damaging free radicals and protect lungs from winter infections, asthma and even the ravages of second hand smoke.
Lemon	Lemons are alkalizing for the body. They are acidic to begin with but they are alkaline-forming on body fluids helping to restore balance to the body's pH. They are rich in vitamin C and flavonoids that work against infections like the flu and colds.

Ingredient	Nutrional Information
Chilli	These hot peppers could burn away some unwanted weight as they raise your temperature! The powerful spice that gives curries their firey taste have been used in almost every culture in one way or another for both culinary and medicinal purposes. It is a versatile medicine and one of it's major uses is as a cardiovascular tonic that enhances circulation. The powerful chemical capsaicin, that gives chilli its perceived heat, has a potent effect on the artery walls. It almost forces a relaxation of the arterial walls causing them to suddenly spasm and then relax. This enhances circulation, especially to our fingers, toes, and even our brain! Chilli is also a painkiller when used topically. The very high vitamin C content can also substantially increase the uptake of non-haem iron from other ingredients in a meal, such as beans and grains.
Mussels	Mussels are a delicious food with a delicate taste. They are high in protein and low in cholesterol and fat. 85g of cooked blue mussels contains 20g of protein and only 147 calories. They are rich in iron, manganese, phosphorous, selenium, zinc and vitamins C and B12.
Limes	Limes have been known to help with diabetes, fatigue, high fevers, various heart disease, colon and prostate cancers.
Onions	As strong in healing power as they are in taste, these vegetables keep infections at a safe distance. Their antibacterial action combat all kinds of infectious diseases which protects the digestive system, reducing the risk of intestinal growths that could lead to more serious diseases. The same compounds cause the smell and healing effects, so the more pungent the onion, the more good it will do! They are packed with vitamin B6.
Cinnamon	Delicious spice that can be used as a sugar alternative to give that 'sweet' taste! A tsp. of cinnamon everyday has been known to reduce sugar cravings and help reverse Diabetes type 2.
Potatoes	Potatoes are one of the least expensive and most readily available sources of vitamin C, a nutrient that is vital for keeping the immune system healthy. New potatoes are richer in this antioxidant than old ones. Most of the fibre which aids digestion and lowers cholesterol is found in the skin.
Mangoes	Mango has the perfect combination of nutrients to protect against premature ageing. It is an excellent source of beta-carotene, the precursor to anti-viral vitamin A and promoting clear skin. Apart from being delicious, mangoes are potent detoxifiers and highly beneficial for the digestive system through their supremely cleansing and soothing properties. They are full of antioxidants, including vitamin E, which is not usually found in fruits, making them one of the most powerful fighters against infection. Packed with vitamin C, mangoes are top detoxifiers, cleansing the blood and kidneys. Eating mangoes improves hair and skin condition. **TIPS: Mango is perfect in fruit salads and desserts, but it works well in savoury dishes too.**
Green Beans	They are a very rich source of dietary fibre which helps to reduce blood cholesterol levels. Green beans contain excellent levels of vitamin A, and health promoting antioxidants. Zea-xanthin is an important dietary carotenoid in the beans that is good for eyesight and offer some protection in preventing age-related macular disease in the elderly.

Ingredient	Nutrional Information
Chicken	Chicken is a good source of the mineral selenium, an infection fighting antioxidant often missing from the diet. Chicken's vitamin B3 and B6 content will help to maintain a healthy nervous system. A useful source of protein, and low fat if the skin is removed, chicken contributes to the growth and repair of all the body's cells.
Mushrooms	Mushrooms have more protein than most vegetables, as well as vitamin E and selenium. Mushrooms are one of the richest sources of a powerful antioxidants which combat cell damage. They are also rich in vitamin B3, (which may slow the onset of age-related dementia), and potassium which helps to regulate blood pressure.
Leeks	An excellent source of dietary fibre and easier to digest than onions. They have anti-septic and anti-arithic propeties. Do not throw out the green part it is packed with nutrition and flavour!
Honey	Honey contains phytonutrients called propolis, which helps to boost immunity and caffeic acid which have anti-carcinogenic properties. This has plenty of anti-aging benefits.
Olive Oil	Olive oil is rich in unsaturated fats. That's the type of fat that helps improve your cholesterol levels and reduces the risk of heart disease and diabetes.
Tomatoes	Most people think of tomatoes as a vegetable when they are in fact a fruit. Made up of 90 percent water, tomatoes are wonderfully hydrating, as well as delicious and versatile, plus they have a low GI and a very low calorie count – perfect for dieters!
Eggs	Protein rich eggs contain all eight essential amino acids helping to make up the building blocks for the entire body, benefitting everything from skin to hair and muscles to bones.
Butternut Squash	They have anti-inflammatory properties that can relieve the pain of many age related conditions. It has a sweet, nutty taste similar to that of a pumpkin.
Basil	Relieves cold symptoms and abdominal and intestinal cramps, improves digestion and refreshes physical energy. Basil leaves are rich in oils that reduce inflammation and kill harmful bacteria. Recent tests have found that these oils can counteract the growth of antibiotic-resistant superbugs, including those that cause food poisoning and others that infect wounds. As it was tradiionally used as an anti-inflammatory remedy, its effects in that area are currently being studied. Around the house, a pot of basil is a traditional insect repellent. **TIPS: Do not refrigerate basil as it will turn black! Add fresh leaves at end of cooking to keep their flavour and their healthy effects.**

Ingredient	Nutrional Information
Prawns	Their selenium content is anti-carcinogenic and essential for heart health. Selenium also fights off wrinkles! Prawns supply iodine, which is vital for the proper functioning of the thyroid gland, and calcium for strong bones. They are also rich in zinc, which boosts immunity and fertility.
Tiger prawns	The world's most popular crustaceans are low in calories and are a great source of protein which is necessary for building healthy tissues. These shellfish are rich in immunity-boosting nutrients and are an excellent source of B-vitamins with youth-enhancing attributes. They are rich in vitamin B12, which promotes brain function and prevents fatigue, and vitamin B3, which is crucial for preserving the memory.
Carrot	This colourful vegetable may not actually make you see in the dark, but it really is good for your eyes and overall vision. The carrot is one of the richest sources of phytonutrients called carotenoids, which are responsible for its colour and for a host of health benefits. These nutrients are what make carrots so good for the eyes, particularly for seeing in poor light.
Rocket Lettuce	This hot, peppery salad leaf is packed with calcium and lots of other essential disease fighting nutrients. Rocket contains high levels of vitamin C, a powerfully antioxidant nutrient that helps to prevent the body against toxins and boosts resistance to viruses and other infections.
Beetroot	Recommended to all sport fanatics. This food is packed with nitric acids that will help keep you going for longer. It is also excellent for your liver. Take some beetroot juice before a marathon or triathalon.
Coriander	Coriander is great for intestinal gas, upset stomach and improving digestion. Recent research shows that it can be used to remove heavy metals from the body.
Aubergines	This is a very low calorie vegetable and has a very healthy nutrition profile. This is good news for dieters and weight watchers! Some people need more iron in their diet, but too much iron isn't a good thing. It increases the body's production of free radicals, byproducts of metabolic processes that damage the cells.
Salmon	Always opt for wild salmon. Farmed salmon has toxins that can be detrimental to your health. Protein rich and packed with Omega 3 fatty acids, Salmon is an excellent food to aid weightloss.
Quinoa	Quinoa is a slow-release energy food originally from South America, the Incas called this the 'mother grain'. Packed full of goodness, it regulates blood sugar, mood swings and cravings. This deliciously nutty flavoured gluten-free grain is very easy to digest and suitable for those with wheat intolerance or coeliac disease. It is a complete protein which means that it contains all eight essential amino acids, an extremely rare quality in the plant world, making it a so-called 'Super Food.' It is an excellent source of antioxidant vitamin E which is needed for the body's healing process. It contains lots of immunity-enhancing minerals including zinc. It also contains lycine which helps fight off viral infections.

Ingredient	Nutrional Information
Avocados	Like the misnomer about tomatoes, avocados are actually classified as a fruit. They are rich in monounsaturated fat that is easily burnt for energy. Avocados increase healthy fat and calorie intake in your diet without seriously increasing your carbohydrate intake. They are excellent for giving your skin a beautiful glow.
Scallops	High in both protein and selenium. They are excellent for aiding with cardiovascular health and protecting against colon cancer.
Garlic	After crushing garlic wait 10 minutes before cooking it to increase its nutritional benefits. Keeping the weight down is just one of this wonder-working bulb's health-enhancing abilities. It is known for its powerful smell and taste, but its protective powers are even stronger, ranging from fighting cancer to promoting weight-loss. Garlic is a 'Slimming Aid'. Allicin is a compound of garlic and has been found to aid weight loss even if you make no other changes to your diet. At the same time, it lowers blood levels of insulin, reducing the risk of weight-related problems such as metabolic syndrome and diabetes. Garlic doesn't just discourage fat from clinging to your hips and thighs, even more importantly, it helps to prevent fatty deposits forming inside your arteries, where they gradually harden and restrict blood flow. People who are trying to lose weight often eat high protein diets and take extra exercise. Add a clove of garlic a day to your diet, as it has been proved to counteract inflammation.
Celery	This is high in Vitamin K and is very useful for soothing the digestive tract. It is a low calorie food that can be enjoyed as a snack with some almond butter.
Thyme	I grow thyme in my front garden and the scent is absolutely divine! Thyme herb contains thymol, one of the important essential oils, which scientifically has been found to have antiseptic, anti-fungal characteristics.
Courgette	Excellent as part of a low calorie diet. Packed with fibre and other beneficial nutrients. Eating a diet rich in vegetables, fruits and other low-energy foods allows you to consume a higher volume of food with fewer calories and less fat.
Lime	High in vitamin C the tangy flesh of lime is an effective immune stimulant. Taking the steps to use lime for weight loss is as simple as adding it to your daily water intake. Lime juices and oils are exceptionally beneficial to the skin. Lime juice, consumed orally, or lime oil, applied topically, rejuvenates skin. Limes keep the human skin healthy, and shiny and helps fight infections. Limes are full of anti-oxidants, anti-biotic, and disinfectants (which means limes also help with acne!) Limes and their anti-oxidant properties help protect your eyes from ageing, and macular degeneration.
Ginger	Ginger is a herb but is often known as a spice, with a strong distinct flavour that can make your mouth water! The Thai don't let their ginger roots grow big. They prefer them smaller, tender and succulent. It's much sweeter and more flavourful that way. Baby ginger (or pink ginger) is excellent for digestion and is excellent for relieving nausea. Try it especially for car or sea sickness. It can also relieve morning sickness in pregnant women! Ginger has a wide variety of effects on the human body and is known to be effective for the treatment of cataracts, amenorrhea, heart disease, migraines, stroke, angina, athlete's foot, colds, bursitis, chronic fatigue, tendinitis, flu, coughs, depression, dizziness, fever, erectile difficulties, infertility, kidney stones, Raynaud's disease, sciatica, and viral infections.
Rice	Always choose brown rice if you are looking for the healthy option. It is richer in nutrients than the white variety. Feeling low or moody? Lift your mood with brown rice, it's dense in B vitamins, which are needed for a healthy brain and nervous system, while its protein levels help to build muscles, skin and hair.